sleep

GRANDPA BILL LIVES ALL ALONE. MRS. BROWN COMES EVERY WEEK TO DO THE CLEANING AND MENDING.

SHE KNOWS WHAT'S BEEN GOING ON. BUT SHE WON'T TALK TO US ABOUT IT WHEN WE VISIT.

sleep

bedtime reading

robert peacock and roger gorman

UNIVERSE

First published in the United States of America in 1998 by UNIVERSE PUBLISHING
A Division of Rizzoli International Publications, Inc.
300 Park Avenue South, New York, NY 10010

Copyright and Compilation © 1998 Robert Peacock and Roger Gorman
A Silent Fable project

98 99 00 01 02/10 9 8 7 6 5 4 3 2 1

Printed in Singapore

Library of Congress Cataloging-in-Publication Data
Sleep : bedtime reading / edited by Robert Peacock and Roger Gorman.   p.   cm.
A collection of over 20 bedtime stories and poems by contemporary
authors accompanied by photographs by contemporary photographers.
ISBN 0-7893-0112-1
1. Sleep—Literary collections. 2. American literature—20th century.   I. Peacock, Robert. II. Gorman, Roger.
PS509.S44S58 1998   97-52939
811'.508'0353--dc21   CIP

contents

DEDICATED TO JERALDINE AND WILMA CLAIRE SOTHERN

Jeraldine Sothern (1934-1997)

For two I have come to know and will always love
–Robert Peacock

AND TO MILES SINCLAIR DUBOIS

Sweet Miles, giving birth to you, I know my strength.
I can do anything! It's a miracle!
You show me too, my weakness, I accept.
My love bursts up and out without warning. You hug me, breath warm on my
neck arms tight about me and it's all I could ever want.
I look on you in sleep, still for a moment finally, then a sigh, a toss and a
turn. I cover you again and wish you the sweetest of dreams.
You dream, I wonder, my milk flows.
I give thanks to the universe, to you, for choosing me as your mother.
Sweet Miles, my son.
–Kelly Sinclair

We would like to give special thanks to Nina Paturel, and acknowledge Sandra Gilbert,

Bonnie Eldon, Charles Miers, Deb Seager, Jenni Holder, Nancy Litnin, Annabel Macrae,

W. M. (Dancing Bear) Hunt, Sarah Hasted, Marvin Heiferman, Carole Kismaric, Carre Bevilacqua,

Susanna Wenniger, Ed Friedman and The Poetry Project, NYC, Laura Young, Leah Sherman,

and Rodney and Sophie Rae McHuge for their support.

Design: Roger Gorman/Reiner NYC

Foreword Robert Peacock

Sleep has two realms, each quite different. There is the realm of the body—in which we rest and replenish ourselves. Then there is the realm of the spirit—the metaphysical, fanciful playground of dreamscapes where the body and soul part ways. Here, we leave convention, reason, and the laws of physics behind. In this realm, the spirit states once again its daily proclamation, "I am here." While our body lies quietly, our mind angles unrestrained through an intricate, sometimes turbulent maze of experience, blessed with the means to realize almost anything. The conscious self gives way to dreams and we enter a world where intellect and reason serve little purpose and imagination dominates. Here the experiences of waking life resurface in strange new forms, bringing with them their incandescent blessings and warnings. Sleep, unburdened by the corporeal, in its deepest and most uncorrupted moments holds the promise of a spiritual partnership with the force that imbues all of life. In its less crystalline form, sleep offers us at least temporal entertainment.

Biologists, philosophers, and theorists have attempted to make sense of sleep. Yet, as important as their studies may be to academia, it is perhaps the less scientific lessons of discovery and divination that sleep delivers—helping us to recognize more clearly what we inherently know.

This unique collection of writings and photography sheds light on this obscure realm of the mind and body where we spend a huge portion of our lives. These authors and photographers prompt us to embrace sleep . . . and at the very least to never underestimate the healing power of the afternoon nap.

Sleep Blessing Tara Johannessen

Take me there.
Promise,

The body understands the

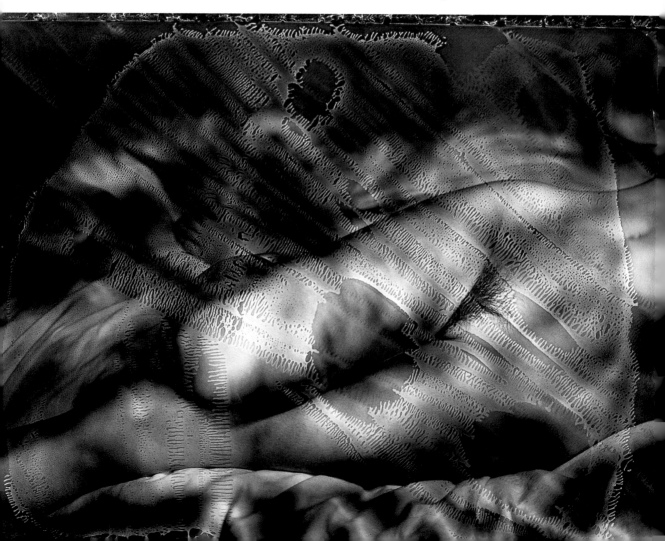

dear shadows

from hope to dark

to the ocean flows.

mind becoming no one.

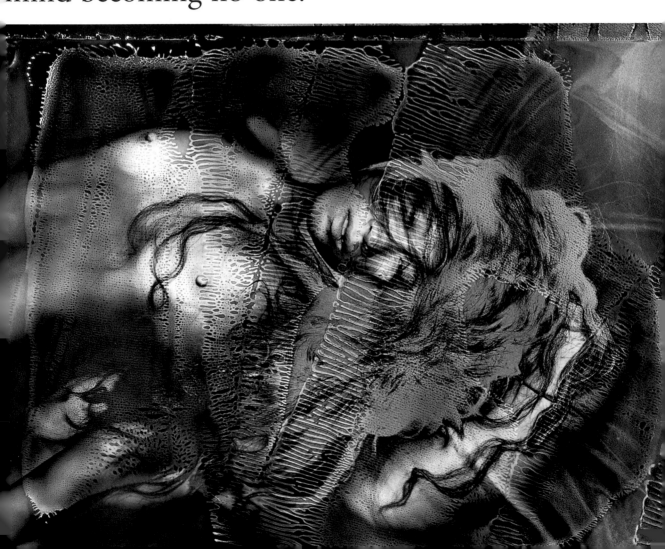

The Blessed Waters of Sleep Andrei Codrescu

These days, I dream of sleep. Sweet narcotic of healing, come to me, I beseech, as I toss restlessly amid the real and imaginary reefs of middle-age anxiety. Come to me with all your cool salves, your chasms, your phantoms, and even your hells! I lie awake, reviewing my life, cursing my doctors, disemboweling my enemies, reinterpreting the once-sweetly simple, climbing the ladder of the never ending list of things to do that will never be done. I think of E. M. Cioran, the great philosopher, who suffered also from insomnia: "And while a world anterior to our waking solicits us, we envy the indifference, the perfect apoplexy of the mineral…" he said. I have tried melatonin, sleeping pills, valerian extract—in vain. I have even tried to buy the sleep of others, convinced that those who sleep more than their share are possessed of a magical substance. As I think of the sleepers, the gifted ones, the young, the unconcerned, sleep recedes even farther. It isn't fair: I, who am a worshiper of dreams, am locked out of the kingdom of dreams, while others, who have neither the vision nor the skill to fully tend their dreams, get to roll like pigs in the treasures of the moon goddess.

duction

It was not always thus. Once, I was a sleepy child in a dreamy city in a slumbering country at the edge of Europe. Romania was steeped in the sleep of centuries, from which history woke it loudly every three decades or so, in order to plunge it into a nightmare of death and destruction. My hometown, Sibiu, in Transylvania, was swathed in layered, thick walls, still sporting moss-covered cannon balls from the countless sieges it endured. Inside these walls we slept, my fellow burghers and I, while the half-lidded, somnolent eyes of attics in the steep roofs, watched over our nights. All of our houses, built in the 13th century, had owls. They perched on trunks full of German encyclopedias, top hats, discarded armor, rolled-up maps. The Pied Piper of Hamlin, it was said, piped the children of Germany over the mountain here, to Sibiu, where they slept.

My kingdom of childhood sleep was vast. I slept in hollows on the dark side of the Teutsch cathedral, I slept on the grass in front of the Astra library, and I slept in school with my head on my schoolbooks, absorbing more of their wisdom than otherwise possible. My favorite book (not a schoolbook) was *A Connecticut Yankee at King Arthur's Court* by Mark Twain. I identified with the Yankee who falls asleep and wakes up in another day and age, where his superior knowledge enables him to control the world. I was certain that just over the threshold of my own sleep lay the world meant for me.

Our great romantic poet Eminescu spun his verses from moon dust and star gossamer. He dreamed tales of stars who fell in love with mortal girls. Spirits, goblins,

ghosts, and old sages populated his verse, freshly arrived from the shores of
Morphia, goddess of sleep. His poetry fed from the dark soil of fairy tales and songs
sung in high mountains beneath sheer walls of granite. The thick forests teemed
with creatures eager to enter our dreams: most of them did so directly, but some
reached us via Eminescu's poetry. Over in England, Keats, Shelley, Byron, and
Coleridge broke open the outer shell of reality's hard nut and let the sweet contents
pour out like a purple fog, bringer of dreams, portents, nocturnal voyages. And over
in America, Edgar Allan Poe, suspended like a question mark of smoke from the
end of his opium pipe, warned the nation of daytime and optimism that a dark
dream, an unseen shroud, stretched just below its sunniness.

The world of sleep is vaster than the world of awakeness. Think of all the
nights that stretch from our frightened, monster-haunted human beginnings to the
loudness of today when we are doing all we can to banish night. We began in the
shelter of the cave, steeped in a nameless dream that had at its center a single flame
whose mystery we have not yet fathomed. What was it that woke us from the essen-
tial sleep of beasts to the odd knowledge that now compelled us to consider our
existence? We awoke from this meditation-dream only when hunger propelled us to
kill, and that was good, because for those few hours we forgot the tormenting flame
and became happily beasts again. Eating well caused insomnia, though, so we
invented song, art, and poetry, to while away the dark. The nights of the neolithic
were long.

The Dream Before

(for Walter Benjamin)

Laurie Anderson

Hansel and Gretel are alive and well
And they're living in Berlin.
She is a cocktail waitress.
He had a part in a Fassbinder film.
And they sit around at night now.
Drinking schnapps and gin.
And she says: Hansel you're really bringing me down.
And he says: Gretel, you can really be a bitch.
He says: I've wasted my life on our stupid legend.
When my one and only love was the wicked witch.

She said: What is history?
And he said: History is an angel being blown
backwards into the future.
He said: History is a pile of debris.
And the angel wants to go back and fix things.
To repair the things that have been broken.
But there is a storm blowing from paradise.
And the storm keeps blowing the angel
Backwards into the future.
And this storm, this storm, is called progress.

Dreamland Mike Dubois

Time lapse in conscious thought, entering the fertile

grounds of slumber.

Slipping into the solitary silence of sleep where once

again the constraints of waking mind surrender to the

unfolding sequence in dreamland where imagination

roams free.

Gone again into shades of familiarity where comfort

resides in knowing that

this is your world exclusively.

Herman Brood

I DON'T SLEEP
I FEAR WAKIN' UP
STRAIGHT
I DON'T WANNA LOSE A
MINUTE
I SHOOT SPEED
I'M OPEN ROUND THE CLOCK
I GIVE ADVICE
I CAN DANCE
NEVER MISS A NEW DAY COMIN'
I DON'T HAVE FRIENDS
I'M 65 YEARS OLD
WITHOUT SLEEP
THAT MEANS
65 X 365 = 9 HOURS
I GAINED
I'M DOIN' WELL
NO SLEEP
COLLECT TIME
DON'T WASTE IT
I'M AN "AINSELGANGER"
THEY CAN'T CATCH ME
SLEEPIN'
I WATCH OVER YOU.

Melody Patti Smith

Her voice was like her name
and when one pointed this out
she would laugh a laugh
equally melodious.
She was an artist's model
so white shouldered
ermine hair, brow
that one saw
black.
a patent pump
erect in snow
she was tho
just a girl
who dreamed
when seven
of riding
a horse
as white as she was
in the center of
a thick swarm
of bees
and slip from
their cloud
unscathed
in a field
of queen anne's
lace
like a great
embroidered cloth
on the table of god
and having said her grace
partake of nothing but honey lent by
that gifted swarm. So enthralled by her
they left behind a coat, a sweet veneer
that left her throat capable of a voice
one could only describe by a name.

Melody.

Her voice was like her name
and when one pointed this out
she would laugh a laugh
equally melodious.
She was an artists model
so white shouldered
ermine hair, brow
that one saw
black,
a patent pump
erect in snow
she was too
just a girl
who dreamed
when seven
of riding
a horse
as white as she was
in the center of
a thick swarm
of bees
and slip from
their cloud
unscathed
in a field
of queen annes
lace
like a great
embroidered cloth
on the table of god
and having said her grace
partake of nothing   but honey lent by
that gifts swarm.   so enthralled by her

gly by? behind in coat, a sweet sneer
that left her throat capable of a voice
one could only mistake by a name.

in My Dream by W.C. Williams

Allen Ginsberg

"As Is you're bearing

a common Truth

Commonly known as desire

No need to dress

it up as beauty

No need to distort

what's not standard

to be understandable.

Pick your nose

eyes ears tongue

sex and brain to show the populace

Take your chances

on your accuracy

Listen to yourself

talk to yourself and others will also

gladly relieved

of the burden–their own

thought and grief.

What began as desire

will end wiser."

The Invention of Solitude (*excerpt*)

Paul Auster

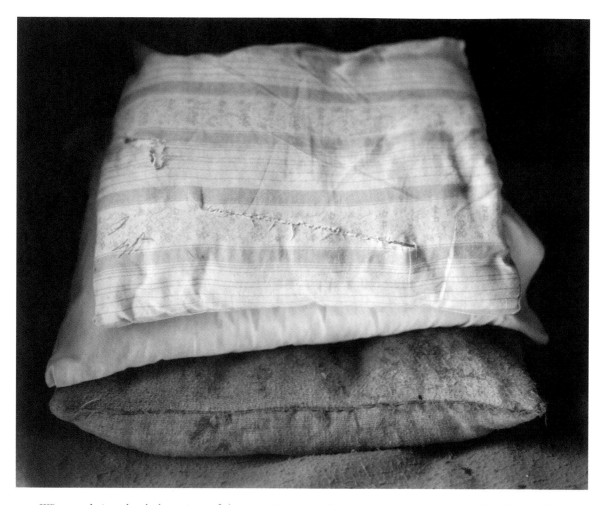

Winter solstice: the darkest time of the year. No sooner has he woken up in the morning than he feels the day beginning to slip away from him. There is no light to sink his teeth into, no sense of time unfolding. Rather, a feeling of doors being shut, of locks being turned. It is a hermetic season, a long moment of inwardness. The outer world, the tangible world of materials and bodies, has come to seem no more than an emanation of his mind. He feels himself sliding through events, hovering like a ghost around his own presence, as if he were living somewhere to the side of himself—not really here, but not anywhere else either. A feeling of having been locked up, and at the same time of being able to walk through walls. He notes somewhere in the margins of a thought: a darkness in the bones; make a note of this.

By day, heat gushes from the radiators at full blast. Even now, in coldest winter, he is forced to keep the window open. At night, however, there is no heat at all. He sleeps fully clothed, with two or three sweaters, curled up tightly in a sleeping bag. During the weekends, the heat is off altogether, both day and night, and there have been times lately when he has sat at his table, trying to write, and could not feel the pen in his hand anymore. In itself, this lack of comfort does not disturb him. But it has the effect of keeping him off balance, of prodding him into a state of constant inner watchfulness. In spite of what it might seem to be, this room is not a retreat from the world. There is nothing here to welcome him, no promise of a soma holiday to woo him into oblivion. These four walls hold only the signs of his own disquiet, and in order to find some measure of peace in these surroundings, he must dig more and more deeply into himself. But the more he digs, the less there will be to go on digging into. This seems undeniable to him. Sooner or later, he is bound to use himself up.

When night comes, the electricity dims to half-strength, then goes up again, then comes down, for no apparent reason. It is as though the lights were controlled by some prankster deity. Con Edison has no record of the place, and no one has ever had to pay for power. At the same time, the phone company has refused to acknowledge A.'s existence. The phone has been here for nine months, functioning without a flaw, but he had not yet received a bill for it. When he called the other day to straighten out the problem, they insisted they had never heard of him. Somehow, he has managed to escape the clutches of the computer, and none of his calls has ever been recorded. His name is off the books. If he felt like it, he could spend his idle moments making free calls to faraway places. But the fact is, there is no one he wants to talk to. Not in California, not in Paris, not in China. The world has shrunk to the size of this room for him, and for as long as it takes him to understand it, he must stay where he is. Only one thing is certain: he cannot be anywhere until he is here. And if he does not manage to find this place, it would be absurd for him to think of looking for another.

Lay Down by My Lullaby

Gerard McHuge

The evening calls upon us all,
Another day spent on the lives that we're lent.
The work is done and weariness calls
All of God's children back into their beds,
Lay down their heads.

CHORUS:

Close your eyes, lay down by my lullaby
When your weary and teary and troubled.
Close your eyes, lay down by my lullaby
When your tired and your mind is befuddled.
Close your eyes, lay down by my lullaby
When your sweet soul is sought out by sorrow,
My love leave all your thoughts 'til tomorrow.

The twilight sky comes cold to our eye
As evening hoists up all the fires it flies.
Jewels aflame sing your forgotten name
And stab through the night to your dreamy delight
Twinkling white.

CHORUS:

Leave your strain for what it all means
And glide down the slide of the golden moons' beams.
The firmament is fleeting and fleeing
And all is a scene in some vagabond's dream
So drift clean away…

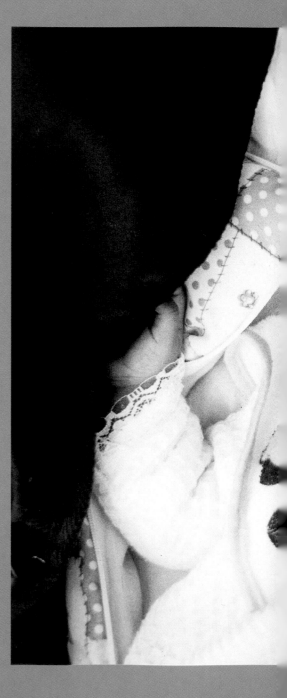

Magritte's Dreams Duane Michals

Magritte dreams of an enormous apple
that fills the room like a giant green balloon.
This plump pippin pushes down the walls
and expands up the hall, then fills the house,
the town, the sky, and everything all around.

Magritte is the seed of the core of an apple universe,
and as he snores he is awakened by the
roar of a deafening crunch.
Someone is eating the apple for lunch.

RENE MAGRITTE ASLEEP

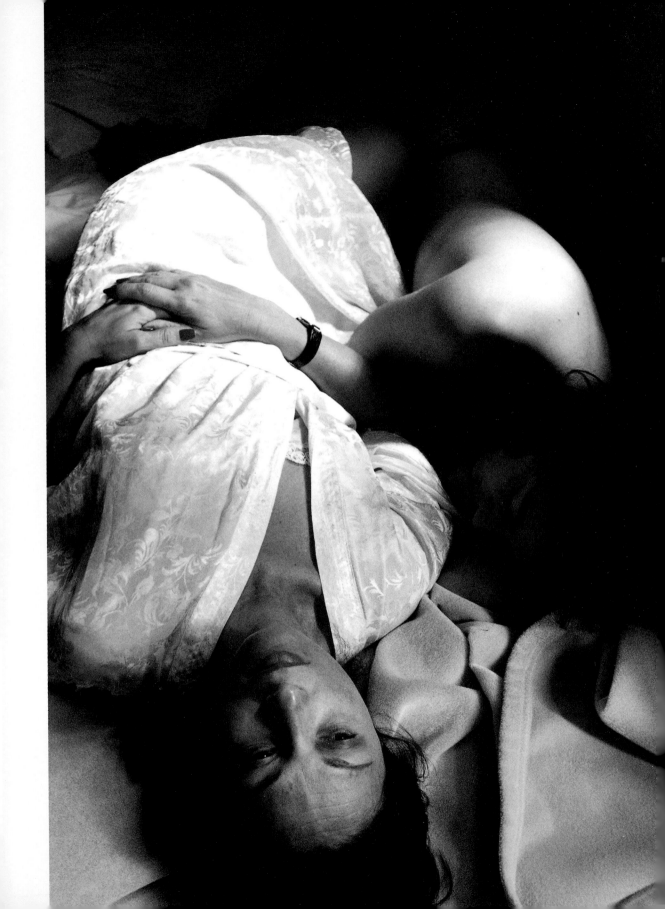

On Dying in Her Sleep

(in which the word love occurs four times)

Kat Blackbird

Maybe it hurt too much to open her eyes.

Maybe she was born to sleep.

Maybe the hope of her heart, to awaken,

fell by accident into her soul,

was intended for some other girl-child.

Tonight it ceased to matter.

Hadn't she made love in the mountains,

hadn't she birthed and raised children

with courage and dignity and even lived,

for years, often happily,

outside of the comfort of a man—

without ever knowing where she was going?

Hadn't it all—

the morning glories on the trellis,

nights of yellow crescent moon

over quiet Ohio cornfields,

those little hand-stitched books she made

or standing bare-footed on hardwood stage floors

in the warm glow of storytelling,

faces smiling and smiling—

hadn't it all been pretty nice?

Perhaps sleepwalking was her fate,

her talent, the tiny seed of frozen fire that,

in spite of thousands of hard lessons on breathing,

would now and forever refuse to break open.

What else could she do but love it as her own,

having come to believe it would not leave

the altar, veiled swirl of mist and fog

centered midpoint between her navel

and pubic bone, just to the front of the brim

of her sacrum. No, this was less than

a matter of a broken heart

or the disjointment of community.

It was just a small ethereal pill:

sleepwalking, day dreaming,

an earth dance done by a woman wanting more,

the drug of desire drawing her on.

Oh, she had also wished for grace,

to let go, to trust, wished and wished.

And do you think that she let go, leaned back

into the arms of what any woman calls love?

Only so far as this—

that tonight she wrote the words

(I know, because I found them): I Love You.

Yes. It all, sound asleep,

still wanting so badly to wake up,

was pretty nice.

Sleep Verlyn Klinkenborg

It is 7:57 A.M. on the Dan Ryan Expressway. A Wednesday. Rush hour. Every minute splits into local and express, and not a single person in Cook County takes the local. The rain beats down. The wind blows. Darkness is piling up toward winter, but the city is hardwired into a different kind of time: market time, phone time, Web time, grid time, tube time, train time, drive time, flight time, bank time, lab time, work time, all of them synchronized, to one degree or another, with atomic time, a second of which, according to the National Institute for Standards and Technology, equals "9,192,631,770 periods of radiation corresponding to the transition between the two hyperfine levels of the ground state of cesium-133." Time slips away at nine billion cesium ticks per second, i.e., continuously. It never sleeps. It asks only of these commuters that they never sleep too. They are trying to oblige, looking out with blood-shot eyes at brake lights as numerous and motile and waterlogged as cranberries in a bog. On the Dan Ryan Expressway it is not yet what you'd call a hyperfine day.

I, too, slept badly again last night. I was in a strange city and in a strange bed filled with the overabundant warmth of a hotel room. At home, I often come awake for an hour or two in the early morning, 3:30, 4:00 A.M. A thread of thought—the merest particle of wakefulness—presents itself and soon the bedside light is on and I'm reading again or lying in the dark, thinking. I often put off going to bed, as I did last night, for no good reason. Like a kid with an eight-thirty bedtime in the eternal twilight of summer, I can't quite bear to quit consciousness. The itch of waking won't subside. This is an old and by now not particularly troublesome habit, though its effects are sometimes tedious and grow more pronounced the older I get. Like almost everyone, I borrow more from sleep than I can ever hope to repay, and I can feel the debt being exacted whenever my attention dissipates. There are days when I wonder what it feels like to be fully awake.

Hearing people talk about their sleeping habits is a little like hearing them talk about their digestion. An unexpected note of pride creeps in, as if the person doing the talking were his own prize county-fair steer. Some persons—a tiny minority—worry that they sleep too much to prosper in these frenetic times. The only individuals who seem content are the ones who cheerfully announce how little sleep they need, and they are often making it up. How we sleep is widely, if implicitly, taken to be an index of things that have little to do with sleep—emotional balance, competitiveness, sensitivity, toughness. Sir Philip Sidney called sleep "the poor man's wealth, the prisoner's release, the indifferent judge between the high and low." But it's easier, I've found, to say what sleep is—to name it metaphorically—than to state what it does or what the widespread effects of gradual, long-term sleep loss in our society might be. Asking what sleep is for sounds like the kind of guileless question philosophers ask, like asking what time is for. It grows curiouser and curiouser the more you think about it.

In fact, it's hard to talk about sleep without talking about time. To see what I mean, imagine a world with no artificial illumination, only the light of day and the dark of night. Imagine, too, that over billions of years organisms evolve that reflect in their bodily systems the relation between light and time in their environment. They develop sensors—eyes—to register the presence or absence of light. They develop internal clocks—genes and cells and clusters of cells capable of generating a biological night and a biological day. They develop pathways along which these sensors and clocks can communicate. Even if light were to disappear for weeks or months at a stretch, the rhythms of biological day and night—circadian rhythms—would still be produced at precise intervals within the bodies of these organisms. Sunrise and nightfall recalibrate the internal clocks of these creatures, so that in winter their biological night is long and in summer it is short. Call this life on earth 40,000 years ago.

Now imagine one such organism with the temerity to light up the night. It fashions lamps of pitch, animal fat, petroleum, inert gases. It ignores what its cells still remember, that light—even artificial light—has the power to regulate biological clocks. It begins to pretend that every night is a midsummer's night only a few hours long. A society full of beings like this would be able to accomplish remarkable things with the extra time it had on its hands. It could build mighty cities and vein those cities with numbered interstates and clot those interstates with automobiles every morning and evening. It could erect eminent bodies, like the Sleep Research Society and the American Sleep Disorders Association and the American Board of Sleep Medicine and the Society for Research on Biological Rhythms. It could foster scientists and physicians whose working lives were spent studying the interactions between light, time, and sleep. But what it would never, ever be able to do again is turn out the lights and roost when the chickens roost.

The one thing this society seems to have wanted all along was to stay up way past its evolutionary bedtime. But the clock we're trying to fool is our own clock, our inherent circadian rhythms. Ultimately, a "clock" is a weak metaphor for the power of those rhythms, which control, among other things, the timing of variations in body temperature, cardiovascular rates, and the secretion of substances like melatonin in the pineal gland, prolactin and human growth hormone in the pituitary, and cortisol in the adrenal gland. Taken as a whole, these variations define not only the internal state of our bodies but also the condition of consciousness itself.

As long as sleep was considered little more than an interruption of the waking state, it was treated as a convenient window through which to view the dreaming mind. Being interested in sleep was just a different way of being interested in consciousness. Much of the early sleep research in this century was based on the assumption, as one biologist put it, that "humans had potentially evolved out of the constraints of the environment." But what if, as seems increasingly apparent, that turns out to be impossible? What if the environment is inescapable? What if sleep is a physiological product equivalent to consciousness and not just a state of suspension in which the mind is suddenly untrammeled? For one thing, most common-sense notions about the relation between sleep and waking fall apart.

In fact, the very idea of circadian rhythms has the effect of uniting waking and sleeping into a single, carefully equilibrated system, so that it becomes impossible to ask what sleep is for without asking what waking is for. It also becomes impossible to imagine that humans have somehow escaped the evolutionary imperative of their environment. Circadian rhythms attune the human organism to the external environment, but they also coordinate the internal operations of the body. To argue that humans have somehow evolved away from the constraints of their environment ignores the fact that the human body is always to a certain extent producing its environment, a bodily environment that is extraordinarily stable, as it is in all mammals.

The circadian system—of which sleep, like the full moon passing across the night sky, is only the most visible marker—is an enormously subtle means of integrating environmental input with a complex suite of physiological outputs. And it is philosophically alarming. Just when you get used to the idea that sleep is a physiological artifact of the circadian system, you realize that waking—consciousness—is not merely the transparent state of being it seems to be. It too is being generated by the body's circadian rhythms. It has a shape and a hormonal substrate all its own. This isn't news, but discovering its truth is a little like the moment when you first realize that the eye is not a window, even into the soul, but an organ with its own opacity. It makes you wonder.

From Position Ed Friedman

The limits of time
Whatever your intentions
Are unrequited
For as little as all
The inches you travel
I can dream a whole life
And come upon it
With lantern held up
Leaning so far forward
As not to need more steps
Only to end up
Go further on

Now I am Dead Quentin Crisp

Now I am dead
the cold square house is shocked
Where once I used to live and wonder why
and every dark uncurtained eye
though bleak before is now a tone more bleak

upon the blue green lawns the starlings struck
where once I stood and hoped that I might die
the strut and lance with sudden beak
the blue green blades that no one comes to cut

and on the pathways tended now no more
the raindrops gathered on the underside
of leafless boughs
drip as they dripped before
and here I walk and wonder why I died.

Night: Recurring Dream

(Direct from My Dream Diary)

Kate Pierson

We are in a beautiful and intriguing forest. I say it is beautiful here and there is a white ring around the moon. There is a tree with arrowheads covering all the branches, like a thorn tree, very beautiful rare and exotic. I look across the field and the landscape is soft and sunset colors are in the sky. I ask which woods shall we go into? I decide to go into the soft dark deep part of the woods where it is unexplored and inviting–I am mystified and filled with wonder.

Wild Kingdom Mark Van de Walle

Tonto hawks and spits, squints up into the setting sun, hawks and lets fly again. Lotta dust out here in the desert. Rough on the throat, the delicate mucous membranes. You want a place on the water when you get old, he thinks, you gotta be a front man. You gotta be a star. You're not a star, and you get the Ed McMahon Residence for Former Professional Associates—that's the official name, but

everybody calls it the Old Sidekicks Home, or just the Home, for short—a very long way indeed from Malibu and the beach. The Home is a wooden island in the middle of the desert, a multi-story clapboard pile that smells of bad directions and failing memories and flop sweat. It was constructed at some indeterminate point between the World Wars, which means it's old enough to be ancient in California. Ed bought the place in the early '70s as a hedge against his own eventual retirement, and then just clean forgot about it in the tide of money that came from his ascension to frontman (*Starsearch*, apparently, was enough to get you into the bigs, much to the chagrin of the Home's residents). So now it was just moldering away in the desert, generating tiny sums of money from tiny payments made from the residents' incredibly tiny pension funds.

Tonto thinks about the Man in the Mask, undoubtedly sitting on his deck chair and watching the sun go down over the Pacific at that very moment, a margarita clutched in each hand. He was always a two-fisted drinker; and he always made the same joke about how it was the only way the Lone Ranger could avoid drinking alone. The joke was lost on his former sidekick, who thought that if the Lone One had sprung for a drink now and again, he maybe could've had some real company when he got plowed. Nowadays, Tonto wears a T-shirt that says, "Fuck You, Kemosabe." He's never been sure what the famous address means exactly—he's Italian himself, a transplant from Brooklyn in the 30s, forced into faux-Indianhood by an olive complexion and the kind of insurmountably thick local dialect that makes it tough to get parts that call for a lot of talking. But still, he feels like the T-shirt pretty much sums up his relationship with his former boss. One of the peculiarities of local manners is that residents don't talk too much about the frontmen: no one likes to be reminded that he's not only a has-been, but in actual point of fact, a never-really-was. For the same reason, the residents mostly use their stage names—every little bit helps.

Tonto leans back in his chair, spits again, watches the wind whip up miniature tornadoes around the billboard of McMahon's smiling face. Be time to repaint Ed soon, he thinks; the toothy mug of the world's most famous sidekick is fading fast, just like everything else out here. Then Tonto pricks up his ears, straining to hear—the wind is suddenly carrying something new, along with the usual cloud of dust. It's the thunder of hoofbeats. It's a hearty Hi Yo Silver awaaa— No, it's not either that. It *is* footsteps though. Going on and on, a steady, ragged drumbeat—it sounds like…

It's the guy in room 109 again. The saddest sack of all the sad sacks at the Home. Whatsisname. Jim. Jim. Former sidekick for that nature show guy, Mervin, Merlin, Marlin, something like that. The ex-Faithful Companion can't quite bring it to mind; there's just this image of silver hair and a frontman's usual shiny smile and a jingle: "Muutuaaal of Oomahaaa— People you can count on when the going's rough…" And then he remembers: *Wild Kingdom.* That's it. From the people you can count on. Count on…Right. Years of faithful service, and Jim winds up here, velcroed to a bed amidst the tumbleweeds, the washed out and the dried up, yelping stuff in his sleep. Screaming. Tonto had listened (and then watched, nobody noticing his presence, a gift for invisibility shared by all second bananas) while they checked him in. At first he was going on and on about cattle prods, and killing Marlin, and later, literally, about lions and tigers and bears oh my. Terrible, terrible. More than bad enough.

But the running was the oddest part of the whole thing. Hard to fathom even for old Tonto, who by then considered himself a pretty hard case, and fairly experienced in the myriad symptoms of bitterness, the side-effects of side-kicking: he never stopped running. Never ever. He was running when they brought him into the home three years ago, unconscious and held up by an orderly on each arm, blood on his safari jacket and hat askew. Like a Roadrunner cartoon: the guy's motoring along in midair, heading full speed off the edge of the cliff, safe as long as he doesn't look. Except in this case, it was pretty obvious that gravity had already won—Jim had already gazed too long into his personal abyss, and now he was screaming down, down. Down… Later, up in his room, strapped into his bed (restrained, management claims, for his own protection), Jim sprinted on in his unnatural sleep, scrawny little pipecleaner legs churning the sheets, beating the air, getting him nowhere fast. His feet drummed the bed when they moved him for feeding, pounded out paradiddles when they slid the bedpan into place. He is a human Energizer Bunny, skinny pink limbs endlessly powered by one-hundred-percent pure remembered fear.

Needless to say, none of this behavior has done much to endear Jim to the staff at the Home. The orderlies all hate him, weirded right out by the brute force of his fear, the strength of his dark dreaming. So occasionally they'll mess with him, sort of accidentally-on-purpose, doing stuff like letting him off his leash when he seems really amped up (but still eerily nonresponsive), and then standing back, watching him career from one side of his room to the other, bouncing off the padding they've installed over the walls, producing muffled thuds on impact. Eventually, he'll knock himself off his feet, fall down and flail around for awhile, looking like nothing so much as some kind of huge, emaciated beetle, unable to heave itself off its back. The orderlies like that bit the best: Hey, they say, it's NutBall. Tilt, NutBall. Tilt.

Tonto figures that if it weren't for the dismaying prospect of losing a steady stream of fat insurance-company checks (and maybe—probably—some hush money thrown in too, since, if it ever got out, Jim's sorry state wouldn't exactly be a public-relations coup for the guys at Mutual) management would have given him the boot ages ago. He kind of likes the guy though, hangs out in the room from time to time, watching him go. The Runner never seems to notice the former Indian's there, just keeps going on and on.

Now, Tonto listens to Jim's drumming heels, lets his chair fall back down on the old wood porch, coughs more dust, and ambles back inside the Home. Sunset, he thinks. Magic time. The crack between worlds. Good time to pay a visit to the Running Man. He ghosts past some of the guys playing cards (Mr. Greenjeans cheating the orderlies blind again, go Greenie, a brief, silent cheer of solidarity), slides up the stairs, down the hall.

He's barely inside the door of room 109 when he realizes something's different: the running. It's stopped. For the first time in three years, the runner pauses. And there's a voice. Floating out of the darkness, not quite a croak, not quite a wheeze, a voice that carries the echoes of something horrible in its quavers. The voice says: "Run, Jim, run. Hah. Moron." Then there's a long pause. A silence. It threatens to engulf the room. Tonto just stares, frozen inside the doorway. "Sancta merda," he breathes, reverting, in his surprise, to the blasphemies of his childhood. "Holy shit."

The voice comes again; it's Jim. Jim says: "My legs hurt."

This proves to be too much for Tonto: he actually breaks down laughing. Just flat out cracking up, shoulders shaking, chest heaving with whacking great gales, peals, gusts, torrents of laughter. Going and going until the tears start from the corners of his eyes, until poor resurrect-

ed Jim catches it, too, and both of them are going. Until finally, the two men are all but howl-
ing in the padded room, Tonto rolling on the floor and Jim thrashing on his bed, laughing and
laughing in the sepulchral twilight of room 109.

    It's a long time before Tonto manages to shake the tears from his bleary eyes, wheeze out
the question that's been nagging at nearly everyone at the home for three years. "Man, what the
hell happened to you?"

    Jim's voice floats down from the bed, weak from laughter and disuse, all but disembod-
ied: "Marlin," he croaks. "And the bear." Which is enough to start both of them up all over
again; that goes on until Tonto pulls it together enough to ask the obvious question: "Bear?"

    "In Montana. Grizzly in Montana. I was on a horse and Marlin was in the helicopter.
Filming." Jim stops, swallowing to lube vocal cords all but rusted solid from disuse. The room
is silent for awhile until he gets going again. "I rode for awhile. The helicopter was 350 feet
overhead, going whup whup whup. Marlin was yelling on a bullhorn. Yelling directions— Left.
Right. Straight ahead. Just yelling. Such a moron."

    Still on the floor, but sitting up now, Tonto spits out a word: "Frontmen." It sounds
like an oath. Like a curse. It echoes. Reverberates in the air. If his grandmother had been
there, she'd have made the horns, warding off possible evil-eye ricochets from the depth of
hatred there.

    "We were out looking for grizzlies in Montana. Mother and cubs—you know. Cute.
Marlin always liked the babies. Good for ratings. He was up in the helicopter with the camera crew.
Couple of hundred feet up in the sky. I was down on the ground. On a horse. The horse was
trained to deal with bear encounters. So I thought everything would be okay. Which it was, until
we actually found a bear." He paused again. "They're the biggest predator on the North American
continent, did you know that? Claws and teeth like butcher knives. And fast, too—forty-plus on
the straightaways. Turns out that horses are terrified of them. Even this trained one. When we
flush the bear out, the horse panics. Throws me and runs. Then bear starts coming for me…"

    His voice is a whisper by now, swallowed up by layers of padding and darkness (no one
turns on the light in the Running Man's room, another one of management's little economies)
just drifting down. "I make it to a tree. Which is useless, because the bear can climb the tree.
Or just knock it over. But playing dead just didn't seem like an option. So while I'm up there…I
realize…I'm dead."

    Then there's another silence. Jim's lost in his memories now, Tonto realizes, ghosting
down the corridors that brought him here, back along the trail that turned him into the Runner.

At last, he surfaces. "I should have been, too. But I guess I got lucky, the grizzly was tired or full or something. Because eventually he went away instead of killing me. And I didn't die. But the thing that really got to me…I mean…while I was in the tree, Marlin was on the loudspeaker. Three hundred feet up in the air, cackling to the crew about what great footage he's getting and yelling "run, Jim, run." Marlin was always yelling that: "run, Jim, run."

Tonto remembers his own years with the frontman: remembers making the coffee every morning and mixing the cocktails every night for twenty-some odd years (and not one damn martini, not a single cosmopolitan for him); remembers the fabulous babes—blondes and brunettes and redheads, all the flavors—who invariably threw themselves at the Masked Man and ignored his own Mediterranean good looks; remembers brushing down Silver after every hard day on the set while the boss was shacked up with the aforementioned cuties. Down on the soft floor, Tonto nods. Tonto understands.

"That was the worst. But there were other times, too. The crocodile down in the Everglades. Marlin swore it was an alligator. They're a little sluggish once they get out of the water. So he sent me out to the shore in my hip boots. Gave me a chunk of raw meat, started the cameras rolling. He said: Wave the meat around. Let it get the smell of blood. And I remember thinking, smell of blood? It was definitely a bad idea. Especially on Marlin's say-so. Anyway, it was a huge croc, not an alligator. Twenty feet long if it was an inch, and it went like lightning out of the water. Like lightning. Right after me and the crew. You can see the camera bouncing around like crazy in the footage. And in the background you can hear Marlin, and he's going—"

Tonto nods his head and finishes it for him: "Run, Jim, run."

They both sit there for awhile, two men in a pitch-black room, looking back. Just breathing together. After awhile, Tonto makes a decision. He heaves himself up to his feet. One hand slides down inside his boot, looking for a familiar shape, pulling it free. A light is beginning to gleam in his eyes, whirling slow and maybe a little crazy. A light that looks as though he, too, has finally awakened from a dream. "Lissen," Tonto says, crossing over to the bed. "I've got something to give to you. It was my grandfather's straight razor, he used it back in the old country to shave his face every day. And maybe for cutting a few other things, too. You know." He's got the blade loose now. "There's something I always wanted to do, the whole time I was with the fucking Ranger. Something I should'a done. Except I couldn't." The crazy light's getting brighter now, even Jim can see it, shining in the ex-Indian Tracker's eyes. "But you. Look at you, man. Anyone can see you're something special. You're the fucking Running Man—three years out cold and you never stopped. Never."

"I couldn't stop," murmurs Jim. "Couldn't. Marlin wouldn't let me. It was Marlin wants this, Marlin wants that, for *seven years*. Every day. For seven years." Jim says, hands still strapped behind his head, but his feet silent (just twitching, every now and then, remembering) against the sheets at last. "And every time there's a baby animal on screen, Marlin gets to cuddle it. I like the babies, too."

Tonto's getting close now, turning eyes like headlights into Jim's. "Exactly, man. Exactly. You suffered. That's what second bananas do." He stops talking, leans down close. Jim sees the razor in his hands now, flashing silver in the dawn's half light. Cutting his bonds, feet first and then the hands. "But you're the Running Man. You're not like the rest of us. Not anymore. So it's gotta be you. Gotta be. All you have to do is run. Just a little bit more. Just  one more time. For all of us." Tonto's pressing the ancient straight razor into Jim's hand.

Jim's legs tremble, fingers curl around the blade. His voice is a sleepy child's, scarcely able to believe that the dream is over. "And then I can stop. One more time, and then I can stop." He looks up into the Indian's eyes. And falls into the light that's there.

Tonto hardly sees Jim move, but he's gone just the same. He's down the stairs, past the orderlies, out into the desert dawn. Running again, feet eating up the desert and the dust and the miles. He is naked speed with a blade in its hands, a cheetah, a wolf pack, a grizzly bear.

He is heading west, toward Malibu and the beach.

Back in room 109, Tonto bares his teeth, laughing. Whispers to an empty room. "Run, Marlin. Run."

Tunnels of the Broadway Bridge Brian Wood

A dream dreamed again and again until I made this picture then never dreamt again. From boyhood then: waking into sweated sheets; walking in a sweat of blood. On a bridge: cement piers plowing up a smooth muscled river. Silted, blistering currents pulling silently through our town, the hissing aftertaste every mother's nightmare. Death-river whispering to young bodies.

Across the bridge. Halfway across. Looking over. A cat is the end of my arm; scratching, tearing, dragging me over. Fighting to shake its searing eyes pulling mind ripping under I'm buried in flesh.

It is my arm.

Writhing, harrowed bone. Dismember me tear me twist me inside out, pull water up into the sky: claws rip at sucking marrow hold onto the sky rushing away and hammer that wedge of stone down into your heart's throat to gut and kill and love till it stops. Then it's gone; a woman gyres slowly to the river as if rising.

Quantum leap to the end of the bridge sloping up toward a dark sky: an empty bridge moonlit and silent, my right foot fixed at the center of a white-chalked circle, just the radius of my left leg's reach.

I cannot move.

A man comes from the other side, each step covers half the distance left, slow yet quick as light, no time passed; suddenly close on my face, my father. His hand raised, he plunges a knife in my thigh, lunging into my reaching flesh, a boar's tusk buried to the lips.

Instantly out from this hot pouch, this thigh, I'm born and up in a twisting flight of feathers.

When She Sleeps

Kristy Lee Vieira

When she sleeps
She is innocent
She has excepted all trouble
When she sleeps
She is at peace
She is rested
When she sleeps

When she awakes
She will no longer be innocent
She will have all her troubles back
When she awakes
She will no longer be at peace
She will have the weight of the world on her shoulders
She will still be rested
When she awakes

She can do things she wants and me as a
big sister can do nothing.
It's upsetting at times but I get through it. She may look perfect
but nobody is. She can be evil at times but then calms down.
She knows nothing
about life yet but she will learn.
She is easy to love especially when she
sleeps.

Nettle and Lilac

Chrystina Bleu

Rock-a-bye-baby I am
a pyro-
maniac baby I been burnin

nettle and lilac
in an ashtray
in my bed by myself ('bye

'bye 'bye myself) I am
a pyro-
maniac baby I been burnin

nettle and lilac yeah
yeah nettle and lilac yeah

yeah nettle
to tackle the nets of
all my small
unnecessary rigidity um hmm and

lilac
for gettin back
my atavist,
elastic mindset and
cut myself come slack yeah
cut myself some slack Rock!

Rock-a-'bye
Rock-a-'bye baby I am
a pyro-
maniac baby I been burnin

nettle and lilac yeah
yeah nettle and lilac yeah and

I am turnin
and tossin
the ashes out of
my Ninth Avenue bedroom window
OHHHHH YEAH! and

the NYC Wind She's
a friend of mine Honey She's takin up my ashes
and She's blowin
the hell outta them (and then She)

re-turns them to me
in a lighter form: I am Re-born: I am

a Firebird Risin from
Dust in the Wind! is the cremation

of my baby's addictions and my
kickass woman's reincarnation I am

a Firebird Risin from
Dust in the Wind Woman! I am

re-vampin my germs like only
A Woman Can Rock!

Rock-a-'bye
Rock-a-'bye baby I am

a Firebird Risin
a Firebird Risin from

a pyro-
maniac baby bur-bur-burnin

nettle and lilac yeah
yeah nettle and lilac yeah I am

a Firebird Risin
a Firebird Risin from

a pyro-
maniac baby bur-bur-burnin

nettle and lilac yeah
yeah nettle and lilac yeah

yeah Firebird Risin!
F (higher) bird Risin um hmmm

Firebird Risin!
     F (higher) bird Risin! (bet your ass I'll
          sing it again: I am)

Firebird Risin!
F (higher) bird Risin! (singin)

Firebird Risin!
F (higher) bird Risin! (singin)

Um um hmmm ummmmmmm hmmmmmmmm!

Night Women Edwidge Danticat

I cringe from the heat of the night on my face. I feel as bare as open flesh. Tonight I am much older than the twenty-five years that I have lived. The night is the time I dread most in my life. Yet if I am to live, I must depend on it.

Shadows shrink and spread over the lace curtain as my son slips into bed. I watch as he stretches from a little boy into the broom-size of a man, his height mounting the innocent fabric that splits our one-room house into two spaces, two mats, two worlds.

For a brief second, I almost mistake him for the ghost of his father, an old lover who disappeared with the night's shadows a long time ago. My son's bed stays nestled against the corner, far from the peeking jalousies. I watch as he digs furrows in the pillow with his head. He shifts his small body carefully so as not to crease his Sunday clothes. He wraps my long blood-red scarf around his neck, the one I wear myself during the day to tempt my suitors. I let him have it at night, so that he always has something of mine when my face is out of sight.

I watch his shadow resting still on the curtain. My eyes are drawn to him, like the stars peeking through the small holes in the roof that none of my suitors will fix for me, because they like to watch a scrap of the sky while lying on their naked backs on my mat.

A firefly buzzes around the room, finding him and not me. Perhaps it is a mosquito that has learned the gift of lighting itself. He always slaps the mosquitoes dead on his face without even waking. In the morning, he will have tiny blood spots on his forehead, as though he had spent the whole night kissing a woman with wide-open flesh wounds on her face.

In his sleep he squirms and groans as though he's already discovered that there is pleasure in touching himself. We have never talked about love. What would he need to know? Love is one of those lessons that you grow to learn, the way one learns that one shoe is made to fit a certain foot, lest it cause discomfort.

There are two kinds of women: day women and night women. I am stuck between the day and night in a golden amber bronze. My eyes are the color of dirt, almost copper if I am standing in the sun. I want to wear my matted tresses in braids as soon as I learn to do my whole head without numbing my arms.

Most nights, I hear a slight whisper. My body freezes as I wonder how long it would take for him to cross the curtain and find me.

He says, "Mommy." I say, *"Darling."*

Somehow in the night, he always calls me in whispers. I hear the buzz of his transistor radio. It is shaped like a can of cola. One of my suitors gave it to him to plug into his ears so he can stay asleep while Mommy *works.*

There is a place in Ville Rose where ghost women ride the crests of waves while brushing the stars out of their hair. There they woo strollers and leave the stars on the path for them. There are nights that I believe that those ghost women are with me. As much as I know that there are women who sit up through the night and undo patches of cloth that they have spent the whole day weaving. These women, they destroy their toil so that they will always have more to do. And as long as there's work, they will not have to lie next to the lifeless soul of a man whose scent still lingers in another woman's bed.

The way my son reacts to my lips stroking his cheeks decides for me if he's asleep. He is like a butterfly fluttering on a rock that stands out naked in the middle of a stream. Sometimes I see in the folds of his eyes a longing for something that's bigger than myself. We are like faraway lovers, lying to one another, under different moons.

When my smallest finger caresses the narrow cleft beneath his nose, sometimes his tongue slips out of his mouth and he licks my fingernail. He moans and turns away, perhaps thinking that this too is a part of the dream.

I whisper my mountain stories in his ear, stories of the ghost women and the stars in their hair. I tell him of the deadly snakes lying at one end of a rainbow and the hat full of gold lying at the other end. I tell him that if I cross a stream of glass-clear hibiscus, I can make myself a goddess. I blow on his long eyelashes to see if he's truly asleep. My fingers coil themselves into visions of birds on his nose. I want him to forget that we live in a place where nothing lasts.

I know that sometimes he wonders why I take such painstaking care. Why do I draw half-moons on my sweaty forehead and spread crimson powders on the rise of my cheeks. We put on his ruffled Sunday suit and I tell him that we are expecting a sweet angel and where angels tread the hosts must be as beautiful as floating hibiscus.

In his sleep, his fingers tug his shirt ruffles loose. He licks his lips from the last piece of sugar candy stolen from my purse.

No more, no more, or your teeth will turn black. I have forgotten to make him brush the mint leaves against his teeth. He does not know that one day a woman like his mother may judge him by the whiteness of his teeth.

It doesn't take long before he is snoring softly. I listen for the shy laughter of his most pleasant dreams. Dreams of angels skipping over his head and occasionally resting their pink heels on his nose.

I hear him humming a song. One of the madrigals they still teach children on very hot afternoons in public schools. *Kompè Jako, domé vou?* Brother Jacques, are you asleep?

The hibiscus rustle in the night outside. I sing along to help him sink deeper into his sleep. I apply another layer of the Egyptian rouge to my cheeks. There are some sparkles in the powder, which make it easier for my visitor to find me in the dark.

Emmanuel will come tonight. He is a doctor who likes big buttocks on women, but my small ones will do. He comes on Tuesdays and Saturdays. He arrives bearing flowers as though he's come to court me. Tonight he brings me bougainvillea. It is always a surprise.

"How is your wife?" I ask. "Not as beautiful as you."

On Mondays and Thursdays, it is an accordion player named Alexandre. He likes to make the sound of the accordion with his mouth in my ear. The rest of the night, he spends with his breadfruit head rocking on my belly button.

Should my son wake up, I have prepared my fabrication. One day, he will grow too old to be told that a wandering man is a mirage and that naked flesh is a dream. I will tell him that his father has come, that an angel brought him back from Heaven for a while.

The stars slowly slip away from the hole in the roof as the doctor sinks deeper and deeper beneath my body. He throbs and pants. I cover his mouth to keep him from screaming. I see his wife's face in the beads of sweat marching down his chin. He leaves with his body soaking from the dew of our flesh. He calls me an avalanche, a waterfall, when he is satisfied.

After he leaves at dawn, I sit outside and smoke a dry tobacco leaf. I watch the piece-worker women march one another to the open market half a day's walk from where they live. I thank the stars that at least I have the days to myself. When I walk back into the house, I hear the rise and fall of my son's breath. Quickly, I lean my face against his lips to feel the calming heat from his mouth.

"Mommy, have I missed the angels again?" he whispers softly while reaching for my neck.

I slip into the bed next to him and rock him back to sleep.

"Darling, the angels have themselves a lifetime to come to us."

Tossing and Turning John Updike

The spirit has infinite facets, but the body
confiningly few sides.

There is the left,
the right, the back, the belly, and tempting
in-betweens, northeasts and northwests,
that tip the heart and soon pinch circulation
in one or another arm.

Yet we turn each time
with fresh hope, believing that sleep
will visit us here, descending like an angel
down the angle our flesh's sextant sets,
tilted toward that unreachable star
hung in the night between our eyebrows, whence
dreams and good luck flow.

Uncross
your ankles. Unclench your philosophy.
This bed was invented by others; know we go
to sleep less to rest than to participate
in the twists of another world.
This churning is our journey.

It ends,
can only end, around a corner
we do not know
we are turning.

sleep

Sleeping with the Snails

Graham Parker

That afternoon, I stopped in a tiny village in the south of France where a fat man named Jacque plied me with red wine and cognac in the dank, pungent bar of the local bistro. Later, half drunk and drowsy from the heat, I met two girls in the village square who dragged me off to a field to watch their lusty, hairy-assed boyfriends playing soccer. Noting the red acoustic guitar dangling from my back, the girls insisted I sing Cat Stevens' songs and the obligatory 'Suzanne' by the dreaded Leonard Cohen. "Bugger the French," I thought, as I made it back to the road and stuck out my thumb.

Eventually, I picked up a lift from a dapper fellow named Didier and after nightfall he dropped me at a dark, dark junction, the language barrier between us giving no clue as to where I was other than pointing in the general direction of Spain. There were no street lamps and suddenly no traffic and I stumbled forward convinced that I was on a small country road until exhaustion took over and I moved off the tarmac and onto a grassy verge where I unrolled my sleeping bag, crawled inside, and fell asleep.

I walked into the quartz room where a quartz budgerigar lived in a quartz cage. I took a pair of quartz scissors from a quartz podium and cut through the quartz cage and the quartz budgerigar and then inspected the quartz floor and the quartz windows that opened out onto a quartz world.

Stepping through the quartz door, I entered not the quartz world, but the Arabic

boudoir of the Turban Man, the curly-toed mustachioed devil with the hookah and the chillium and all the rest of his hashish paraphernalia. He invited me to hit the pipe and we swam together in a paisley, insignia-drenched inner plateau rich with musk derived scents and devoid of Cat Stevens' music. But then the fuzzy-faced sneak began playing footsie with me, wriggling those silken, purloined Mandarin's shoes against my sweaty bare feet.

I spun awake, as if astral traveling out and above the astral I had been in and into the astral of the flesh where I awoke to intense French morning sunlight, the reek of gasoline and a roar of engines. I lifted my head from the ex-army sleeping bag as muddy, garlic breathing French lorry drivers leaned from the cabs of their *thundering* vehicles and gave me odd, quizzical smirks or sarcastic toots of their horns.

I was surrounded by a pounding, deafening cacophony of traffic! I had fallen asleep on a grassy traffic island in the middle of a major motorway! Not only that, a *slimy* track ran across my head and dozens of similar glistening paths traversed my sleeping bag and at the end of each, making its sticky way back into shelter of the grass, was a brightly colored snail.

Like Buddha, I had gone into the void (albeit a cluttered, quartzy, Turbany void), sustained the wet crawling of gastropods and awoke, back in the world of dreams, back in a crazed, gasoline-drenched Frenchness after a damn weird night's sleep.

That to the Sides of the Dark Shine the Theories Richard Hell

Yesterday, late in the evening, I started feeling thick and heavy as if I were being pulled down, as if something deep underground had started to exert a new kind of gravity that was sucking my body and senses towards it, while my floating mind stayed above. I could hardly keep my eyelids raised and I had to lie down. Once I did that, my body hollowed and lightened, like a drawing of itself. My mind seemed to be cut loose, it leaked into my body like molecules: sex, sox, six, sax, sux.... It was like my body liquefied, then evaporated, the whole prehistoric breathing, and my mind was a rudderless little boat that drifted in it. I seeped and haltingly flowed according to the permeability and slant. In the puddles at the bottom of the boat was a tumbled messy litter of everything imaginable that had happened or could happen to me. How could it be so small? My senses seemed to have returned, but were caught in the contents of the boat, as if perception were engendered by those animating objects.[1] It seemed that if I looked at one item—a tan-colored lifesize hobbyshop model of a robin, for instance—everything else in the strew became possible, so that when my attention left the glued-together plastic bird, the items around it had become something other than what they'd been before. Oh, it was too beautiful, this surrender. It is the secret standard of worthiness. All who do it are good! My mind[2] opened and the boat, being one, the only, wasn't a boat.[3]

---

[1] Later I heard "that to the sides of the dark shine the theories."*

[2] If the brain-neurons are buzzing, are individual, can choose, aren't they all of life and history? Each person is God and the brain's neurons are all the people of the history of the world. We are the neurons in God's brain. (Is God asleep? Will God awake? And then what happens to us? God's wakefulness the laws, God's sleep the activity.)

[3] Somewhere in the ocean I started getting an erection. Marilyn Monroe had a penis. The boat sprang a leak. I "woke up"** with come all over me.

These Days

Some Words for People I Think of as Friends

Alice Walker

These days I think of Belvie
swimming happily in the country pond
coating her face with its mud.
She says:
"We could put the whole bottom of this pond in jars
and sell it to the folks
in the city!"
Lying in the sun she dreams
of making our fortune, à la Helena Rubenstein.
Bottling the murky water
too smelly to drink,
offering exotic mud facials and mineral baths
at exorbitant fees.
But mostly she lies in the sun
dreaming of water, sun and the earth
itself—

Surely the earth can be saved for Belvie.

These days I think of Robert
folding his child's tiny shirts
consuming TV dinners ("A kind of *processed* flavor")
rushing off each morning to school–then to the office,
the supermarket, the inevitable meeting: writing,
speaking, marching against oppression, hunger,
ignorance.
And in between having a love affair
with tiny wildflowers and gigantic
rocks.
"Look at this one!" he cries,
as a small purple face
raises its blue eye to the sun.
"Wow, look at that one!" he says,
as we pass a large rock
reclining beside the road.
He is the man with child
the new old man.

Brushing hair, checking hands, nails
and teeth.
A sick child finds comfort
lying on his chest all night
as do I.

Surely the earth can be saved for Robert.

These days I think of Elena.
In the summers, for years, she camps
beside the Northern rivers
sometimes with her children
sometimes with women friends
from "way, way back."
She is never too busy to *want* at least
to join a demonstration
or to long to sit
beside
a river.
"I will not think less of you
if you do *not* attend this meeting," she says,
making us compañeras for life.

Surely the earth can be saved for Elena.

These days I think of Susan;
so many of her people lost
in the Holocaust. Every time I see her
I can't believe it.
"You have to have some of my cosmos seeds!"
she says
over the phone. "The blooms
are glorious!" Whenever we are together
we eat a lot.
If I am at her house
it is bacon, boiled potatoes,
coffee and broiled fish:

if she is at my house it is
oyster stew, clams, artichokes
and wine.
Our dream is for time in which
to walk miles together, a couple
of weeds stuck between our teeth,
comfy in our yogi pants
discoursing on Woolf
and child raising,
essay writing and gardening.
Susan makes me happy
because she exists.

Surely the earth can be saved for Susan.

These days I think of Sheila.
"'Sheila' is already a spiritual name," she says.
And "Try meditation and jogging both."
When we are together we talk
and talk
about The Spirit.
About What is Good and What is Not.
There was a time she applauded my anger,
now she feels it is something I should outgrow.
"It is not a useful emotion," she says. "And besides,
if you think about it, there's nothing worth
getting angry about."
"I do not like anger," I say.
"It raises my blood pressure.
I do not like violence. So much has been done to me.
But having embraced my complete being
I find anger
and the capacity for violence
within me.
Control
rather than eradication
is about the best

I feel I can do.
Besides, they intend to murder us,
you know."
"Yes, I understand," she says.
"But try meditation
and jogging *both;*
you'll be surprised how calm you feel."
I meditate, walk briskly, and take deep, deep breaths
for I know the importance of peace to the inner self.
When I talk to Sheila
I am forced to honor
my own ideals.

Surely the earth can be saved for Sheila.

These days I think of Gloria.
"The mere *sight* of an airplane puts me to sleep,"
she says.
Since she is not the pilot, this makes sense.
If this were a courageous country,
it would ask Gloria to lead it
since she is sane and funny and beautiful and smart
and the National Leaders we've always had
are not.
When I listen to her talk about women's rights
children's rights
men's rights
I think of the long line of Americans
who should have been president, but weren't.
Imagine Crazy Horse as president. Sojourner Truth.
John Brown. Harriet Tubman. Black Elk or Geronimo.
Imagine President Martin Luther King confronting
the youthful "Oppie" Oppenheimer. Imagine President
Malcolm X going after the Klan. Imagine President Stevie
Wonder dealing with the "Truly Needy."
Imagine President Shirley Chisholm, Ron Dellums or
Sweet Honey in the Rock

dealing with Anything.
It is imagining to make us weep with frustration,
as we languish under real estate dealers, killers,
and bad actors.

Gloria makes me aware of how much we lose by denying,
exiling or repressing parts of ourselves
so that other parts,
grotesque and finally lethal
may creep into the light.
"Women must seize the sources of reproduction," she says,
knowing her Marx and her Sanger too.

Surely the earth can be saved for Gloria.

These days I think of Jan,
who makes the most exquisite goblets
–and plates and casseroles.
Her warm hands steady on the cool
and lively clay,
her body attentive and sure, bending over the wheel.
I could watch her work for hours—
but there is never time. On one visit I see the bags
of clay. The next visit, I see pale and dusty molds,
odd pieces of hardening handles and lids. On another,
I see a stacked kiln. On another, magical objects of use
splashed with blue, streaked with black and red.
She sits quietly beside her creations
at countless fairs
watching without nostalgia
their journeys into the world.
She makes me consider how long
people have been making things. How wise
and thoughtful people often are.
A world without Jan would be like her house
when she is someplace else—gray, and full of furniture
I've never seen before.

Our dream is to sit on a ridge top for days
and reminisce
about the anti-nuke movement.
The time we were together
at a women's music festival, and Diablo Canyon
called her.
The more comic aspects
of her arrest.

There is a way that she says "um *hum*" that means a lot
to me.

Surely the earth can be saved for Jan.

These days I think of Rebecca.
"Mama, are you a racist?" she asks.
And I realize I have badmouthed white people
once too often
in her presence.

Years ago I would have wondered
how white people have managed to live
all these years
with this question
from their children;
or, how did they train their children
not to ask?

Now I think how anti-racism
like civil rights or
affirmative action
helps white people too.
Even if they are killing us
we have to say, to try to believe,
it is the way they are raised,
not genetics,

that causes their bizarre,
death-worshiping
behavior.

"If we were raised like white people,
to think we are superior to everything else
God made, we too would behave the way
they do," say the elders.
And: "White folks could *be* people of color
if they'd only relax."

Besides, my daughter declares
her own white father "Good," and reminds me
it is often black men
who menace us on
the street.

Talking to Rebecca about race almost always
guarantees a headache.
But that is a small price
for the insight and clarity
she brings.

Surely the earth can be saved for Rebecca.

These days I think of John, Yoko and Sean Lennon.
Whenever I listen
to "Working-Class Hero,"
I laugh: because John says "fucking"
twice,
and it is always a surprise
though I know the record by heart.
I like to imagine
him putting Sean to bed
or exchanging his own hard,
ass-kicking boots
for sneakers.

I like to imagine Yoko
making this white boy deal with the word **NO**
for the first time.
And the word **YES** forever.
I like to think of this brave
and honest
new age family
that dared to sing itself
even as anger, fear, sadness and death
squeezed its vocal cords.

Yoko knows the sounds of a woman coming
are finer by far than those of a **B-52**
on a bombing raid.

And a Kotex plastered across
a man's forehead at dinner
can indicate serenity.

> *Hold on world*
> *World hold on*
> *It's gonna be all right*
> *You gonna see the light*
> *(Ohh) when you're one*
> *Really one*
> *You* get *things done*
> *Like they never been done*
> *So hold on.*[*]

Surely the earth can be saved
by all the people
who insist
on love.

Surely the earth can be saved for us.

[*]From "Hold On John" by John Lennon

A Previously Unpublished Dream

Jack Kerouac

JUMPING INTO THE TROLLEY on a rainy night in Frisco, on Broadway going down to the Barcadero, that same location dreamed before as in bright sun of sea-going day now's in the drizzle of the Hilltop Frisco Russian Hill Dream when I stopt on top during a long walk and suddenly felt the awful spectrality of "all of us" being there on Russian Hill—I get in the trolley behind a sailor just as the conductor has walked back 5 paces to joke with the rear man, I sit down (normally, not cheating) like a flash behind the sailor's walking figure and just then the conductor turns and sees only the sailor getting in and doesn't even notice me and I've saved a dime—which I think "I might as well" do, remembering past savings like this—I'm working, because later I'm in my room, workclothes all over, ben workin with Joe McCarthy across the hot dusty infantry fields carrying enormous dufflebags—When our day is through we see another batch of soldiers lounging on tufts of earth near the barrier of the official Army grounds and the big buildings— "You the boys from Cranford I sent for?" says Mac—"Yes sir"—"Report at 10 o'clock tomorrow morning"—I can see they're gonna have a ball tonight but McCarthy who's been struggling all day in impossible travails in the hot sun is only going to allow himself 2 extra hours of sleep and come right back tomorrow—Now, later, I'm riding the work train across the hot dusty flats, playfully dangling one foot near the ground, and thinking "I forgot my money and my Hinayana check in the room?" and thinking "After another week a this and another $55 catch-up I'll go back on the railroad up at San Jose"——but I wake up on my quiet couch of Tao repose realizing I only want a life of inaction and adventure every day—

The '56 Chevy

Richard Tayson

I like to think it was baby
blue, I like to see my
father begin the weekly
burnishing, his hands
wringing out the chamois
cloth, smooth as a baby's
skin. He moves it in slow,
precise circles over the left
headlight, that glass eye
like the eye of a man who has
drunk too much and is staring.
He presses his palm to the hood,
tenderly, with steady pressure,
he opens the door to clean
the interior, white as my mother's
skin. I like to think he paid
so much attention to her, that he
danced with her that night, Ink
Spots, Drifters, "Smoke Gets in
Your Eyes," I like to see him
press my mother's young body
to his and their first
kiss I wish to believe was given
in passion. He loved the pure
white of her eyelet dress, the open
sepals where her skin showed through
as they danced slow. And when
she lay down in the fleshy stomach
fat of the back seat, he told her
he loved her, undoing
the clasp at her neck, quick hitch
of the cummerbund's calyx.

And then I do not like to think of it,
I feel a pain deep in my body
where my seeds are made, I feel
discomfort when I say she
must have closed her eyes
and gone back to her step-father
coming into her room, weekly, to lay
his long adult body over that
child, my mother. I wonder
if she drifted up, away
from her bed and over the house,
into the deep blue above Gardena,
finally coming to rest in my father's car.
The seed caught inside her, and I
like to think I had consciousness
even then, the single cell of my being
absorbing the taste of tequila
from their mouths, stars
like blinking chromosomes
above the high school parking lot.
And when he drove her home,
I like to think I sat with them
to be sure he didn't swerve
over the edge of the soft
shoulder and down into
the blue water, I like to think
I stayed in the car
after they've left it,
I lie in the back seat and feel
the leather mold to my body,
the exact point of conception.

Dreamin': Escape Lou Reed

If I close my eyes I see your face and I'm not without you
If I try hard and concentrate I can still hear you speak
I picture myself in your room by the chair
you're smoking a cigarette
If I close my eyes I can see your face you're saying, "I missed you"
Dreamin'—I'm always dreamin'

if I close my eyes I can smell your perfume you look and say, "Hi babe"
If I close my eyes pictures from China still hang from the wall
I hear the dog bark I turn and say, "what were you saying?"
I picture you in the red chair inside the pale room

You sat in your chair with a tube in your arm–you were so skinny
You were still making jokes I don't know what drugs they had you on
You said, "I guess this is not the time for long term investments"
You were always laughing but you never laughed at me

They say in the end the pain was so bad that you were screaming
Now you were no saint but you deserved better than that
From the corner I watched them removing things from your apartment
But I can picture your red chair and pale room inside my head

If I close my eyes I see your face and I'm not without you
If I try hard and concentrate I can hear your voice saying
"Who better than you"
If I close my eyes I can't believe that I'm here without you
Inside your pale room your empty red chair and my head
Dreamin'. I'm always dreamin'

A Childhood Friend Grows Up

Jules Shear

Writing songs is really what I do with my life but that doesn't mean it's easy. In fact, despite being fairly unsociable, I've known other songwriters along my path who've suffered the maddening struggle of dragging these creations out of themselves. Many try co-writing, hoping that the other person will be the dragger and themselves, the more enviable draggee. But for those, like me, who prefer the solitary agonies, we must invent that co-conspirator.

Stories abound concerning writers and alcohol. Drugs are an obvious muse, but with dire longtime consequences. More benign but every bit as eccentric are writers who must use their lucky pen or that guitar that apparently has all those songs in it. It does seem to help though if your crutch is a little bad for you. Then you're really working.

Fortunately, for me, when I was a child, sleep was sloth. It meant you were wasting the constructive parts of your life where what really mattered occurred. But I loved to sleep as much as possible and my dad yelling to get my lazy butt downstairs to help him with some household chore only magnified that love.

So now I have made it necessary to what I do with my life. I've become convinced over the past few years that I only write my best in the few hours just after I wake from a long night of sleep. I don't know why it works. Maybe fresh from dreams, my mind makes those tenuous connections that songs require. Maybe it's simply that I'm well rested. But I've developed a deeper appreciation for my childhood friend with whom I supposedly spent too much time waiting to be an adult.

Now when I'm in a groove of working on songs for a project, I enjoy a one hour nap around four in the afternoon. It seems to work as well as eight hours at night and waking up twice a day, I get twice as much done. Bliss is a siesta. The guilt only helps.

By the way, my lucky pen is a uni-ball fine point.

The Taxi Ride

Jane Siberry

it's clear to me now
i understand
a jump of cards
in an idle man's hand
ohhh…you're sleeping
this is the story
of your leaving

i can win you with reason
i can make you agree
the way that i love you
it only makes sense
that you love me
but down through the sad facts
i'm sifting
you did not think this
without help from me

i've called a taxi
it's coming at dawn
i said send the best one
it's a long, long, lonely ride
to find the perfect lover
for your lover
and the morning light is breaking

i thought i heard someone screaming outside
but it was just a bus pulling away

love is a strange thing
it depends what one gives
and sometimes to give means
give someone away
ohhh… you're sleeping
the same sad pillow
said you're leaving

i move with your breathing
i breathe with your beauty
your sweet heaviness
your deep voice your soft neck
i press my face
did you call me?…
it's only the trees outside flailing
it's only the sirens that are wailing

hurry up driver
you're going too slow
can't you go faster
it's a long, long, lonely ride
to find the perfect lover
for your lover
and the morning light's just breaking

and then you realize you are alone
and your skin against the cold
metal of awareness you fall into
a deeper dreamless slumber and
a stranger enters the room and
is struck by the transparency of
your cheeks and then your arms
and hands and wonders at the
waxen figure and walks out again
the stranger walks out into the
street watching cars pass and
people cross and scenery change
he sees a palm frond thinks how
ugly–is surprised by the violence
of the thought looks again at it
feels nothing and walks on

a deep and dreamless slumber
where only the slow pulse
in the waxen temples keeps vigil

Another Queendom

Esther H. Voet

A full moon crosses the sky, changes shadows through the curtains.

Breathing in out, in out.

She wonders off into a world of oblivion,

a strange place she doesn't know of: the black whole of her existence.

Suddenly she's back and wonders through a fairytale queendom.

Breathing in out, in out.

Isis says hello, fear comes and goes,

colours change and her soul speaks: gives riddles for her to unwind

A far away world awakens, King Sun conquers the sky.

Breathing in out, in out.

He changes the shadows through the curtains.

She opens her eyes to the one she loves: a new life is waiting.

Why I Love to Sleep Fran Lebowitz

I love sleep because it is both pleasant and safe to use. Pleasant because one is in the best possible company and safe because sleep is the consummate protection against the unseemliness that is the invariable consequence of being awake. What you don't know won't hurt you. Sleep is death without the responsibility.

The danger, of course, is that sleep appears to be rather addictive. Many find that they cannot do without it and will go to great lengths to ensure its possession. Such people have been known to neglect home, hearth, and even publishers' deadlines in the crazed pursuit of their objective. I must confess that I, too, am a sleeper and until quite recently was riddled with guilt because of it. But then I considered the subject more carefully and what I learned not only relieved my guilt but also made me proud to be among the fatigued.

I would like to share my findings so that others might feel free to lay down their once uplifted heads. I have therefore prepared a brief course of instruction in order to instill pride in those who sleep.

The Fran Lebowitz Sleep Studies Program

Sleep is a genetic rather than an acquired trait. If your parents were sleepers, chances are that you will be too. This is not cause for despair but rather for pride in a heritage that you share not only with your family but also with a fine group of well-known historical figures. The following list is indicative of the diversity to be found among sleepers:

Some Well-known Historical Figures Who Were Sleepers:

Dwight D. Eisenhower. While many remember Ike (as he was affectionately called by an adoring nation) for his golf, there is little doubt but that he was a sleeper from childhood, a trait he unquestionably carried with him to the

White House. In fact, so strongly committed was he to sleep that one could barely distinguish Ike's sleeping from Ike's waking.

William Shakespeare. Known as the Bard among his colleagues in the word game, Shakespeare was undoubtedly one of literature's most inspired and prolific sleepers. Proof of this exists in the form of a bed found in the house he occupied in Stratford-upon-Avon. Further references to sleeping have been discovered in his work, and although there is some question as to whether he actually did all his own sleeping (scholarly debate currently centers around the possibility that some of it was done by Sir Francis Bacon), we are nevertheless safe in assuming that William Shakespeare was indeed a sleeper of note.

e.e. cummings. The evidence that e.e. cummings was a sleeper is admittedly sparse. Therefore, it is generally accepted that he was perhaps more of a napper.

It is only to be expected that if so many well-known historical figures were sleepers, their accomplishments should be of equal import. Following is a partial list of such achievements:

Some Contributions to World Culture Made by Sleepers
Architecture
Language
Science
The wheel
Fire

I rest my case.

Text Credits:

9. Foreword by Robert Peacock, 1997. 10. Tara Johannessen, *Sleep Blessing*, 1996. Courtesy of the Author. 12. Introduction by Andrei Codrescu, *The Blessed Waters of Sleep*, 1997 © Silent Fable. Courtesy of Silent Fable. 16. Laurie Anderson, *The Dream Before (for Walter Benjamin)*, 1989. Reprinted by permission of the Author. 18. Mike Dubois, *Dreamland*, 1997. Courtesy of the Author. 21. Herman Brood, *Untitled*, 1997. Courtesy of the Author. 24. Patti Smith, *Melody*, 1994. Courtesy of the Author. 26. Allen Ginsberg, *Written in My Dream by W. C. Williams,* from *White Shroud: Poems 1980-1985* by Allen Ginsberg, 1986. Reprinted by permission of HarperCollins Publishers, Inc. 28. Paul Auster, *The Invention of Solitude* (excerpt). From *The Invention of Solitude* by Paul Auster, 1982. Penguin, USA. Reprinted by permission. 30. Gerard McHuge, *Lay Down by My Lullaby*, 1996. Courtesy of the Author. 32. Duane Michals, *Magritte's Dreams*, 1997. Courtesy of the Author. 35. Kat Blackbird, *On Dying in Her Sleep (in which the word love occurs four times)*, 1997. Courtesy of the Author. 36. Verlyn Klinkenborg, *Sleep*, 1997. Courtesy of the Author. 43. Ed Friedman, *From Position*, 1994. Courtesy of the Author. 44. Quentin Crisp, *Now I am Dead*, 1952. Courtesy of the Author. 47. Kate Pierson, *Night: Recurring Dream (Direct from My Dream Diary)*, 1997. Courtesy of the Author. 48. Mark Van de Walle, *Wild Kingdom*, 1997. Courtesy of the Author. 55. Brian Wood, *Tunnels of the Broadway Bridge*, 1997. Courtesy of the Author. 57. Kristy Lee Vieira, *When She Sleeps*, 1997. Courtesy of the Author. 58. Chrystina Bleu, *Nettle and Lilac*, 1997. Courtesy of the Author. 60. Edwidge Danticat, *Night Women,* from *Krik? ›Krak!* by Edwidge Danticat, 1995. Reprinted by permission of Soho Press, on behalf of the Author. 65. John Updike, *Tossing and Turning*, from *Collected Poems 1953-1993* by John Updike, 1993. Reprinted by permission of Alfred A. Knopf, Inc. 68. Graham Parker, *Sleeping with the Snails*, 1996. Courtesy of the Author. 70. Richard Hell, *That to the Sides of the Dark Shine the Theories*, ©1997 by Richard Meyers. Courtesy of the Author. 72. Alice Walker, *These Days,* from *Horses Make A Landscape Look More Beautiful* by Alice Walker, 1983. Reprinted by permission of Harcourt Brace & Company. 82. Jack Kerouac, *A Previously Unpublished Dream,* from *Book of Dreams*, by Jack Kerouac, ©1997 by John Sampas. Reprinted by permission of Sterling Lord Literistic, Inc. 84. Richard Tayson, *The '56 Chevy,* 1993. Courtesy of the Author. 87. Lou Reed, *Dreamin': Escape*. Words by Lou Reed. Music by Lou Reed and Mike Rathke. 1992 Metal Machine Music. All Rights Controlled and Administered by Screen Gems-EMI Music Inc. All Rights Reserved. International Copyright Secured. Used by Permission. 88. Jules Shear, *A Childhood Friend Grows Up*, 1997. Courtesy of the Author. 91. Jane Siberry, *The Taxi Ride*, 1985. Reprinted by permission of Red Sky Music/Wing It Music. For more information on Jane Siberry: www.sheeba.ca 93. Esther H. Voet, *Another Queendom*, 1997. Courtesy of the Author. 94. Fran Lebowitz, *Why I Love to Sleep*, 1975. Reprinted by permission of William Morris Agency, Inc., on behalf of the Author.

Photographic Credits:

Front cover; Pavel Banka, *The Ladder*, 1986. Courtesy of the Artist. 1. Rocky Schenck, *The Visiting Kids*, 1987. Courtesy of the Artist. 2. Chris Verene, #A, from the *Grampa Bill* Project, Printed 1997. Courtesy Vaknin/Schwartz Gallery, Atlanta, Georgia. 4. Christina Dimitriadis, *Private Spaces: Berlin/Bedroom*, 1995. Courtesy of the Artist. 7. Craig J. Barber, *Succulent Gate*, 1988. Courtesy of the Artist. 8. William Christenberry, *Cabin, Shiloh Battlefield, Tennessee*, 1967. Courtesy PaceWildensteinMacGill, New York. 10-11. Osaka Hiroshi, *Venus #30*, 1990. Courtesy Picture Photo Space, Osaka, Japan. 15. Karekin Goekjian, *Harmony*, 1990, Courtesy of the Artist. 17. William Wegman, *Untitled*, 1992. Courtesy PaceWildensteinMacGill, New York. 18-19. Zabo Chabiland, *Matsuda*, 1992. Courtesy of the Artist. 20. Judy Coleman, *Aura,* 1988. Courtesy of the Artist. 22. John McWilliams, *Dupree Road*, 1986. Courtesy of the Artist. 23. Ruth Leitman and Steve Dixon, *Untitled*, 1997. Courtesy of the Artists. 25. Edward Maxey, *Melody*, 1989. Courtesy of the Artist. 26-27. Lynda Frese, *Flesh, Blood, Rain*, 1992. Courtesy of the Artist. 28. Andrea Modica, *Treadwell, New York*, 1996. Courtesy Edwynn Houk Gallery, New York. 30-31. Tim Rollins & KOS, *Pearl*, 1989. Courtesy of the Artist. 33. Duane Michals, *Rene Magritte Asleep*, 1965. Courtesy of the Artist. 34. Elinor Carucci, *Mom and I*, 1995. Courtesy Ricco/Maresca Gallery, New York. 38-39. Sandy Skoglund, *Squirrels at the Drive-In*, 1996. Courtesy of the Artist. 42. Joyce Tenneson, *Old Man and Deanna*, 1986. Courtesy of the Artist. 45. Merri Cyr, *Untitled*, 1994. Courtesy of the Artist. 46-47. Zeke Berman, *Untitled*, 1988, (Web #2). Courtesy Laurence Miller Gallery, New York. 48. Margaret Moulton, *Untitled*, 1990. Courtesy of the Artist. 53. Peter Campus, *Numen/Nineteen*, 1994. Courtesy Paula Cooper Gallery, New York. 54. Jerry Uelsmann, *Untitled*, 1991. Courtesy of the Artist. 56-57. Nancy Burson, *Untitled*, 1996. Courtesy of the Artist. 59. Sally Mann, *Eyeless in Col Alto*, 1993. Courtesy Edwynn Houk Gallery, New York. 64. Petah Coyne, *Untitled #735*, 1994. Courtesy Laurence Miller Gallery, New York. 66-67. Susan Lipper, *Untitled* from *The Grapevine Series*, 1991. Courtesy of the Artist. 68-69. Amy Steiner, *Arizona*, 1995. Courtesy of the Artist. 71. Andres Serrano, *The Morge (Child Abuse)*, 1992. Courtesy Paula Cooper Gallery, New York. 80-81. Laura Levine, *Sinead O'Connor, N.Y.*, 1988. Courtesy of the Artist. 83. Jeffrey Silverthorne, *Untitled*, 1994. Courtesy of the Artist. 85. Pinky /MM Bass, *In Abiquiu (from Dreams of Death)*, 1987. Courtesy of the Artist. 86. Virginia Beth Shields, *Red Dreams*, 1994. Courtesy of the Artist. 89. Rimma Gerlovina and Valeriy Gerlovin, *Absolute Clock*, 1989. Courtesy of the Artists. 90. Nan Goldin, *Amanda on my Fortuny*, Berlin, 1993. Courtesy of the Artist. 92. Mary Ellen Mark, *Acrobat Sleeping, Great Famous Circus, Calcutta, India.* 1989. Courtesy of the Artist. Back cover; Ruth Thorne-Thomsen, *Duet, Wisconsin*, 1991. Courtesy Laurence Miller Gallery, New York.